Confident
Women
Designed by *Almighty God*

Confident
Women
Designed by *Almighty God*

I AM RIGHTEOUSLY RESOLVED TO BE A
CONFIDENT WOMAN OF GOD

CAROL VINSON LEA

WESTBOW·
PRESS
A DIVISION OF THOMAS NELSON
& ZONDERVAN

WestBow Press books may be ordered through booksellers or by contacting:

WestBow Press
A Division of Thomas Nelson & Zondervan
1663 Liberty Drivew
Bloomington, IN 47403
www.westbowpress.com
1 (866) 928-1240

ISBN: 978-1-4908-5906-4 (sc)
ISBN: 978-1-4908-5907-1 (e)

Library of Congress Control Number: 2014956172

Printed in the United States of America.

WestBow Press rev. date: 12/02/2014

Contents

Resolution

I am Resolved to be a Confident Woman of God: Remembering that God is the Source of all things. "Greater is He that is within me than he that is in the World."

I am Resolved to be a Confident Woman of God: Realizing that God's way is the only way. In the natural order of His Creation, there is always harmony, never confusion; always peace, never strife; always abundance, never lack; always good, never evil; always love, never hate.

I am Resolved to be a confident Woman of God: Recognizing that the unity of All things of the people reside in the Sovereignty of God. "The earth is the Lord's and the fullness thereof; the world and they that dwell there in."

I am Resolved to be a Confident Woman of God: Rightly dealing only in truth, honesty, virtue, loyalty, and Christ like love, know that "As ye sow, so shall ye reap."

I am Resolved to be a Confident Woman of God: Relying on the promises of Almighty God that my future will be great as I decide to make it. "I can do all things through Christ who strengthens me" (Phil. 4:13). Therefore, I owe it to myself and the world to become as great as my Creator intended me to be.

I am Resolved to be a Confident Woman of God, and let other group members Confront me in love so that I can grow.

Dedication

This Bible study is affectionately dedicated to the memory of my deceased Mother and Aunts who greatly influenced my life:

My Mother: Lottie Glenn Vinson
My Aunts: Dorothy Glenn Harris and Mary Glenn Sledd

Special Thanks

Special thanks to my children for their love and many ways of encouraging and inspiring me to continue doing what I do:

Tasha LaRae Murdock (God-daughter)
Francois Duvalier Lea, I (Son)
Dr. Claybon Lea, Jr. (Son)

I thank Almighty God and the Mount Calvary Baptist Church for the many opportunities to try my hand at Bible teaching. I thank God for the many churches and civic groups that have invited me throughout the years to share the gift of teaching.

And so, here it is, and somewhat because of all of you, I decided to get out of the boat, and walk on the water.

Forward

CONFIDENT WOMEN: DESIGNED BY ALMIGHTY GOD, I believe, will have a lasting impact upon those who will avail themselves to the applications contained within it.

I have known Carol Vinson Lea since 1982, first from a distance, as the pastor's wife, and later more intimately as the Minister of Christian Education at Mount Calvary Baptist Church of Suisun City, California. It is in this relationship that I came to know Carol as a Christian woman who loves her God and His people.

Carol is the exemplification of a committed, competent and confident Christian woman. She has a "heart" for women's hearts and constantly and consistently offers encouragement to them.

Carol has a refreshingly transparent method of sharing God's Word as is evident in this book. Through her transparency, she challenges women to face their own level of confidence in God. She has been gifted to share God's Word in a way that allows women to feel safe enough to be open and vulnerable, opening the way for spiritual breakthroughs and healing.

Carol continues to serve Mount Calvary's Discipleship Ministry. She not only facilitates Bible studies at her home church, but is a highly sought after speaker at other churches and organizations. How wonderful it is to finally have her, God anointed, teachings compiled into a book so that they are available for untold numbers to be able to learn what God has for them, delivered through Carol.

May you receive all that God has for you, in this study and at the end of the study you, too, are a more committed, competent, Confident Woman of Almighty God.

Fabie Lee Coleman

Introduction

WELCOME to Confident Women: Designed by Almighty God. I am overjoyed that you've chosen to share this journey through Scripture with me. Please be prayerful and honest as we study together.

Through character interpretation, scripture and prayer, this study leads you on a journey to discover or rediscover the confidence within. At the beginning of the study, try to rate your level of confidence on a scale from 1 to 10. At the end of the study, check your level of confidence, and see if you've grown a bit.

Don't forget that you can gain a wealth of knowledge through the sharing of experiences with your sisters who are also engaged in this study. Pay particular attention to the elder women, they have a wealth of wit, charm, wisdom and grace that only age can bring.

This study is designed to be completed over a 6 to 8 week period. The first session is designed to get to know each other and discuss the expectations of the remaining sessions. There will be a total of four sessions. Each session except the first session, will contain five subject matters. There will be a different subject matter for each session and each weeks study. This book provides self-paced, interactive instructions to help you prepare for the weekly small group sessions. Getting prepared for the study is somewhat like getting prepared for a storm.

- Find a quiet place to pray and study
- Keep your Bible, notebook, study guide, pen or pencil available at all times
- You may also choose to study with a friend
- Always conclude your study with prayer

At the end of each week's lesson, I encourage you to ask yourself two questions:

1. Did God speak directly to me today?
2. How do I plan to respond to Him?

We are doing this study to enlighten and help women, through the study of Scriptures to change their minds, hearts and lives. We are also exploring ways that the past has affected the present, and will affect the future. This study is highly recommended for women who want to increase their self-esteem and confidence by following the path God ordained in His divinely inspired Holy Word. This is a great resource to use with Women's Study Groups whether large or small. It can also be used for private study.

God has taught me so very much about Himself and how He has designed women. He has also taught me about myself. As I prepare for retirement this year (2014), in my senior years, I have a greater grasp of the woman I am and still can be. I want to always be a woman after God's own heart, and live up to how He made me. "I will praise thee: for I am fearfully and wonderfully made: marvelous are thy works; and that my soul knoweth right well" (Psalms 139:14). I have made great improvements in my life as a direct result of God's directions. I challenge you to let God do His perfect work in you through this study.

"If I can help somebody as I pass along, then my living will not be in vain."

Carol Vinson Lea

Prayer Time

This Week's Growth Goal

1. You will take steps to begin building your self-esteem
2. You will begin to find self-esteem in Christ

"Therefore, there is now no condemnation for those who are in Christ Jesus, because through Christ Jesus the law of the Spirit of life set me free from the law of sin and death. For what the law was powerless to do in that it was weakened by the sinful nature, God did by sending His own Son in the likeness of sinful man to be a sin offering. And so he condemned sin in sinful man, in order that the righteous requirements of the law might be fully met in us, who do not live according to the sinful nature but according to the Spirit." Romans 8:1-4 (*NIV*)

- By myself there's no way I can keep all of God's rules. According to the Bible, I am a sinner (see Rom. 3:23). I have a sinful nature, a part of me that responds to what is wrong. I do not have the strength within me to do what is right.
- As a disciple of Christ, I am free because Jesus died for me.
- I will experience freedom and confidence as I follow the Spirit of God.

Share Resource Materials

Session Format (time, dates, location and schedules)

Confidence Level Check

> Have each person write down where they believe their confidence level is on a scale of 1 - 10 as a Child of God on this beginning date of Session One. Do this check at the end of the study, also.

Discuss Next Week's Assignment

Closing Prayer

SESSION TWO: CONFIDENT WOMEN OF GOD: PAST, PRESENT AND FUTURE

Day 1:   Who We Are Starts in Our Mind

Day 2:   What Does It Mean to Be a Woman of God

Day 3:   When, Where and Why is Confidence Necessary

Day 4:   Describing a Woman of God: Past, Present and Future

Day 5:   Review, Resolution and Strategies

"being confident of this, that He who began a good work in you will carry it on to completion until the day of Christ Jesus" Philippians 1:6

SESSION TWO: <u>CONFIDENT WOMEN OF GOD: PAST, PRESENT & FUTURE</u>

INTRODUCTION

Women are precious gifts from God to the world. We are creative, sensitive, compassionate, intelligent, talented, and loving. God created man first - but He quickly discovered he needed a helper; not a slave, but a helper. Women ought not ever be walked on, disrespected, bullied, or belittled. Eve was created because Adam needed her.

> *Memory Verse*
>
> *I can do everything through him who gives me strength.*
>
> *Philippians 4:13 NIV*

Since this study is for women, let me hurriedly say - you don't have to be married to be a confident woman of God - enjoy your life and do great things. Philippians 4:11 *(NIV)* says, "I am not saying this because I am in need, for I have learned to be content whatever the circumstances." I am a confident woman of God. I believe confidence is all about being positive concerning your identify - who you are - sure of your salvation - being positive concerning what you can do - and not fretting or worrying over what you cannot do.

A confident woman is open to learning, because she knows that her confidence allows her to walk through life's doorways - eager to discover what waits on the other side. She knows that every new unknown is a chance to learn more about herself and to unleash her abilities and potential.

Confident Women Session Two will address Who We Are Starts In our Own Minds (Day 1), What Does It Mean to Be A Woman of God (Day 2), When & Why is Confidence Necessary (Day 3), Describing A Woman of God, Past, Present, & Future (Day 4), and Review, Resolution, Strategies (Day 5). This session will introduce the connection between our heart, mind, and spirit to that of God, the value of women in the sight of God, provides role models of confident women of God in biblical times, and confident women of God in the past, present, and future. Recognizing the awesome challenge, and responsibility, women will recognize female babies, girls, and teens as our future confident women of God.

SESSION TWO: <u>CONFIDENT WOMEN OF GOD: PAST, PRESENT & FUTURE</u>

DAY ONE: <u>WHO WE ARE: IT STARTS IN OUR MINDS</u>

Les Brown, a Christian motivational speaker likes to say, "Don't allow your circumstances to define who you are." Another way of saying this is "Don't let your condition be your definition." One other quote that we hear often is "as a person thinketh, so he doeth." A friend of mine likes to add, "so a woman thinks, she does and feels." Despite whatever is going on around us, confident women of God choose to view themselves

> *Memory Verse*
>
> *I can do everything through him who gives me strength.*
>
> *Philippians 4:13 NIV*

as phenomenal women, albeit a work-in-progress. According to Harper's Dictionary:

> **mind**, the English translation of various Hebrew and Greek words denoting the human capacity for contemplation, judgment, and intention. As intellect, mind makes possible the critical appraisal and selection of differing opinions. In this sense, mind may also describe one's own mind-set, attitude, or characteristic point of view (e.g., Phil. 2:2-5). In both the Old Testament (OT) and the New Testament (NT), 'heart' is often used as the equivalent of 'mind' and, indeed, is sometimes translated as 'mind' (e.g., Isa. 65:17; Jer. 19:5). In the NT, Paul is especially concerned that the Christian's mind be transformed by a renewed dedication to the will of God (Rom. 12:2).

<u>Please write Philippians 1:6 below:</u>

_____

_____

_____

_____

Remember the Wizard of Oz character Dorothy? Dorothy looked everywhere for her own brain (thinking ability), and her own heart (the courage to pursue her dreams). Our brains are thought to house our minds and hearts is thought to house our feelings. Scientists (neurologists, psychiatrist, psychologists, etc.), philosophers, and theologians study and try to give human understanding to what only God knows for sure. Confident Women of God use God's Word for revelation about God, and themselves.

READ AND FILL IN THE BLANKS:

(We'll use different versions here, so use your own Bibles to make sure we are not making anything up!)

READ: Phil. 1:6 (*AMP*): And I am _____ and _____ this very thing, that He Who began a good work in you will continue until the day of Jesus Christ [right up to the time of His return], developing [that good work] and perfecting and bringing it to full completion in you.

Ans - convinced, sure.

READ: Phil. 12:2 (*HCSB*): Do not be conformed to this age, but be transformed by the _____ of your _____, so that you may _____ what is the good, pleasing, and perfect will of God.

Ans - renewing, mind, discern

READ: Romans 12:3 (*HCSB*): For by the _____ given to me, I tell everyone among you not to _____ of himself more highly than he should _____. Instead, think, _____ as God has distributed a _____ of faith to each one.

Ans - grace, think, think, sensibly, measure

READ: Matthew 22:37, 38 (*HCSB*): He said to him, " _____ the Lord your God with all your heart, with all your soul, and with all your _____ This is the greatest and most important command."

Ans - love, mind.

REFLECTION

1. Who are you in your own mind and how does that compare to God's view of you?
2. What does your faith in Christ Jesus have to do with your mind?

FILL IN THE BLANKS: (Again, we will use different versions, so use your own Bibles to make sure that we are not making anything up!

Memory Verse
I can do everything through him who gives me strength.
Philippians 4: 13 NIV

Phil. 4:13 (*AMP*): I have _____ for _____ things in _____ Who _____ me [I am ready for anything and equal to anything through Him Who infuses _____ into me; I am _____ in Christ's sufficiency].

Ans - strength, all, Christ, empowers, inner strength, self-sufficient

John 15:5 (*HCSB*) "I am the _____; you are the _____. The one who remains in Me and I in him _____ much _____, because you can do _____ without Me.

Ans - vine, branches, produces, fruit, nothing

Phil. 3:3 (*NIV*): For it is _____ who are the circumcision, we who worship by the _____ of God, who glory in Christ Jesus, and who put no _____ in the _____.

Ans - we, Spirit, confidence, flesh

Jerimiah 17:5 (*KJV*): Thus saith the _____; _____ be the _____ that _____ in man, and maketh _____ his arm, and whose _____ departeth from the _____.

Ans - Lord, cursed, man, trusteth, flesh, heart, Lord.

SUGGESTED ACTIVITIES

1. If you have not yet begun to keep a journal for this study, now would be a good time to begin. Note your thinking patterns, note your feelings, and your actions. Note whether your fruit (what you do) is a result of your thinking or feelings, or both. Note whether your mind, heart and strength is congruent. Note whether your actions are according to who you are and whose you are.

2. There are many ways to renew one's mind. Make index cards of scripture that helps you to remember to help you renew your mind. You may want to develop your own categories or use encouragement, praise, sickness, worship, prayer, deliverance, etc. etc. Keep these with you to meditate on in times of either your need or someone else's need.

SESSION TWO: <u>CONFIDENT WOMEN OF GOD: PAST, PRESENT AND FUTURE</u>

DAY TWO: <u>WHAT DOES IT MEAN TO BE A WOMAN OF GOD?</u>

In this section, we will discover what it means to be a woman of God. He is our Creator, the Omniscient, Omnipotent, and Omnipresent One. He is God of all, Lord of lords, and King of kings. He is our Heavenly Father.

Please write Philippians 1:6:

_____

_____

_____

Women, we can find strength and support to solve any problem that will come our way in this life. We can move after pain. As a creation of Almighty God, we have His strength and His power to help us over our weakest hours. We can bloom where we're planted. We can spend more time with our Maker in prayer and study. Proverbs 3:5-6 (NIV) tells us to "Trust in the Lord with all your heart and lean not on your understanding; in all your ways acknowledge him, and he will make your paths straight."

A woman of God seeks to serve, rather than to be served. She looks for ways to help others at home, work, jobs, churches, neighborhoods or wherever she may be. A woman of God seeks to represent her Master. She realizes that there is a time for everything. Seasons do change, and many times in life, it's just not the right time for some things to occur in our lives.

A woman of God is not a complainer. She many times in life has to take bad situations, and find some good in them in order to survive. She praises God with her lips and more with her heart. She is a grateful person, and knows that with God that all things are possible. She is truly a woman of integrity.

The woman of God knows who she is in Christ Jesus. Her confidence is found in God, not in man. I Thessalonians 5:17-18 (*NIV*) tells us to: Pray without ceasing. In everything give thanks: for this is the will of God in Christ Jesus concerning you.

How is your confidence level today?

READ Genesis 1:27-28, and Genesis 22:21-23 & ANSWER THE QUESTIONS

> *Memory Verse*
>
> *I can do everything through him who gives me strength.*
>
> *Philippians 4: 13 NIV*

1. God created females in whose image?

   _____

2. Who blessed females to be fruitful and multiply?

   _____

3. Who brought the woman to the man?

   _____

4. Look at the letters in the words man and woman, and write what you see.

   _____

Confident Women of God, our confidence, certainty, and surety of who we are begins in our minds because we must be sure, certain, and trust that we are children of God. It is with our minds we are able to discern or to make decisions for ourselves based on God's view of us. It is not our nature, it is not our nurture, but rather the nourishment that we receive from God Himself, in Spirit and truth, and through His Holy Word.

Let us pause, here for just a moment, and give Eve her due homage. Eve is often remembered for being tricked into leading humankind into sin. I believe our Omniscient, Omnipresent, Omnipotent Creator knew beforehand what Eve would do. He made her curious, desirous of knowledge, and generous. Did she not want to share with her husband? God desires a love affair with us too. He purposefully designed us with the capacity to make choices. Before we judge Eve too harshly remember we are all works-in-progress until Jesus comes again.

READ: Genesis 3:20; 1 Corinthians 11:17

T/F

_____ Eve was the first mother of all creation.
_____ Eve was the first wife.
_____ Eve was the first and last to sin.

Confident Women of God are children of The Creator, and therefore creative. We are loved by God and love God, and therefore lovers, and we are doers. Confident Women of God can do anything they set their minds to. Say this out loud:

> "I CAN DO ALL THINGS THROUGH CHRIST
> WHO STRENGTHENS ME"
> I AM, THEREFORE, I CAN!
> I CAN ACHIEVE ANYTHING THAT I CAN BELIEVE!

Sometimes, we need to affirm ourselves and not always wait for others to make decisions for our lives or to speak into our lives, to give us approval, .i.e.,

> I CAN LOSE WEIGHT!
> I CAN SAVE MONEY!
> I CAN GO BACK TO SCHOOL!
> I CAN LIVE THIS SINGLE LIFE WITH INTEGRITY!
> I CAN LAUGH AGAIN!

LET'S REVIEW THE SIGNFICANCE OF KNOWING WHO WE ARE IN THE CONTEXT OF OUR OWN MINDS AND THE THEME SCRIPTURE.

Phil. 1:9-11 And this is my prayer: that your love may abound more and more in _____, so that you may be able to _____ what is best and may be pure and blameless until the day of Christ, filled with the fruit of righteousness that comes through Jesus Christ-to the glory and praise of God.

Ans - knowledge and depth of insight, discern

Phil. 1:13 As a result, it has become _____ throughout the whole palace guard and to everyone else that I am in chains for Christ.

<table>
<tr><td>

Memory Verse

I can do everything through him who gives me strength.

Philippians 4: 13 NIV
</td></tr>
</table>

Ans - clear

Phil. 1:18 But what does it matter? The important thing is that in every way, whether from false _____ or true, Christ is preached. And because of this I _____.

Ans - motives, rejoice

Phil. 1:20 I eagerly _____ and hope that I will in no way be ashamed, but will have sufficient _____ so that now as always Christ will be exalted in my body, whether by life or by death.

Ans - expect, courage

Phil. 1:25-26 _____ of this, I _____ that I will remain, and I will continue with all of you for your progress and joy in the faith, so that through my being with you again your joy in Christ Jesus will overflow on account of me.

Ans - convinced, know

Phil. 1:27 Whatever happens, conduct yourselves in a manner worthy of the gospel of Christ. Then, whether I come and see you or only hear about you in my absence, I will _____ that you stand firm in _____ _____, contending as one man for the faith of the gospel.

Ans - know, one spirit

Phil. 1:29 For it has been granted to you on behalf of Christ not only to _____ on Him, but also to suffer for Him,

Ans - believe

WOW! Confident Women of God believe, know, are persuaded, are one in spirit, convinced, expecting, courageous, have self-sufficiency in Christ Jesus. Not only that, we rejoice and suffer as did Christ Jesus.

REFLECTIONS

1. What is the measure of your faith? Does it correspond to your confidence in Christ Jesus to work all things out to His glory?
2. What does it mean to be a Confident Woman of God? Obviously we have our good and bad days or moments, but our hope remains in Jesus.
3. When people are doing good things such as sharing the gospel do you find yourself questioning their motives?

COMPARE Matthew 22:37-38; Deuteronomy 6:5 and Luke 10:27

T/F

_____ Confident Women of God have strength.
_____ Confident Women of God forget to love themselves.
_____ Confident Women of God hold a part of themselves from God.

COMPARE: Romans 8:28; I Peter 2:9 and Ephesians 1:11

T/F

_____ Some things work out for those that love God.
_____ Those that love the Lord have been predestined to do so.
_____ God is worthy of praise.

COMPARE: Hebrews 3:6 to Matthew 10:22 and Romans 5:2

T/F

_____ Confident Women of God hold on to their faith.

_____ Confident Women of God rejoice in the hope of the glory of the Lord.

_____ Confident Women of God are women of faith, grace, and endurance.

SUGGESTED PERSONAL ACTIVITIES:

1. Write to God, thanking Him for keeping you at all times in every situation.
2. Explain to someone what Jesus means to you during the good and bad times.

I, once again declare that I am a confident woman of God. I declare again that I believe I can fly. I am, therefore, I can. Jesus has given me faith by grace to endure. I am an endurer. I am more than a conqueror. God Himself gave me an awesome mind to discern, to know that all things work to the good for those that love Him. I understand that my sufferings are not in vain. I can rejoice in my pain. Whether single, divorced or married, God loves me, and I Him. He is the lover of my soul. There are not enough pages to say what it means to be a confident woman of God. I pray that you are able to understand what it means to be a confident woman of God. You can fly as high as you believe that you can!!!!! Go to school, start a business, stay home with children, whatever. It's your choice!!!

SESSION TWO: <u>CONFIDENT WOMEN OF GOD: PAST, PRESENT AND FUTURE</u>

DAY THREE: <u>WHEN, WHERE, & WHY IS CONFIDENCE NECESSARY</u>

Ladies, we live in a world where children are starving, battered, and sexually abused. Nations are at war. Family members are in conflict. Christians are persecuted for their faith on the job, in the schools, and sometimes even in their own churches! Women still are paid less for doing the same jobs, held back in the corporate world, and vocational ministry work just because they are women. Women who choose to stay home to raise their children, are often psycho-emotionally, and physically abused by their mates, and looked at as fools by their working counterpart females. How many times have you heard, "I thought you were a Christian?" How many times have you wished that Jesus would just come back again now and clear up this mess?

But you are Confident Women of God, a Phenomenal Woman, a righteous woman, a work in progress. Your faith in God makes you a confident woman. You are convinced and fully persuaded. Hold fast to your confidence. We must show confidence in every area of our lives. Confidence is something we decide to have. Let no one take it away from you.

Confident women of God, say aloud, "I can do all things through Christ who strengthens me." Christ strengthens you to be confident. Christ will strengthen you to act confidently. Keep on going!

<u>Please write Philippians 1:6 below:</u>

_____

_____

_____

_____

READ & FILL IN THE BLANKS: ROMANS 8:17, Romans 8:37

Romans 8: 17 (NIV): For in the _____ a righteousness from God is revealed, a righteousness that is by _____ from first to last, just as it is written: "The righteous will _____ by faith.

Ans - gospel, faith, live

Romans 8:37 (NIV): No, in all these things we are more than _____ through him who _____ us.

Ans - conquerors, loved

Reflections

1. Reflect on the circumstances, situations in your present day, in your home, and the community that you live in, and think about how you have or have not shown confidence in Christ?
2. Reflect on the circumstances, situations, and your mother, or another older Christian woman in her present day, or in the past, and think about how she showed or did not show confidence in Christ?

Read Romans 8: Describe the environment, why, and how confidence was displayed?

_____

_____

_____

_____

_____

_____

_____

READ: 1 SAMUEL 30:1-20

From David's point of view, where do we show confidence?

_____

_____

_____

_____

_____

_____

> **_Memory Verse_**
>
> *I can do everything through him who gives me strength.*
>
> *Philippians 4: 13*
> *NIV*

From the captives' point of view, where do we show confidence!

_____

_____

_____

_____

_____

_____

SUGGESTED ACTIVITIES:

1. For the NEXT week practice reframing. Do not say the words "I can't."
2. Often times, we do not act on our own wants, needs, and desires because we doubt our abilities, or because we have never done it before. Pick one thing per day that you have doubt, question, or fear, and take the first step, then the second, third, and so on!

READ: James 1:8 and explain why confidence is necessary?

_____

_____

_____

_____

SUMMARIZE THIS LESSON FOR TODAY

_____

_____

_____

_____

_____

_____

_____

SESSION TWO: <u>CONFIDENT WOMEN OF GOD: PAST. PRESENT AND FUTURE</u>

DAY FOUR: <u>DESCRIBING A WOMAN OF GOD: PAST, PRESENT, & FUTURE</u>

A woman who knows who she is does not sell herself short. A woman who knows that God is her Creator and seeks to find the confidence necessary to fulfill her destiny is a confident woman of God.

<u>Please write Philippians 1:6 below:</u>

Memory Verse
I can do everything through him who gives me strength.
Philippians 4:13 NIV

_____

_____

_____

_____

<u>COMPARE 2 CORINTHIANS 2:14</u>. This time, I'll provide the various translations.

NIV (1984)	KJV	AMP	NLT	HCSB
But thanks be to God, who always leads us in triumphal procession in Christ and through us spreads everywhere the fragrance of the knowledge of him.	Now thanks be unto God, which always causeth us to triumph in Christ, and maketh manifest the savour of his knowledge by us in every place.	But thanks be to God, Who in Christ always leads us in triumph [as trophies of Christ's victory] and through us spreads and makes evident the fragrance of the knowledge of God everywhere,	But Thank God! He has made us his captives and continues to lead us along in Christ's triumphal procession. Now he uses us to spread the knowledge of Christ everywhere, like sweet perfume.	But thanks be to God, who always puts us on display in Christ and through us spreads the aroma of the knowledge of Him in every place.

"being confident of this, that He who began a good work in you will carry it on to completion until the day of Christ Jesus" Philippians 1:6

T/F

_____ Confident Women of God rarely give thanks to God.

_____ Confident Women of God are ministers of a new covenant.

_____ Confident Women of God are captives to the world.

_____ Confident Women of God preach a ministry of life or death.

_____ A Confident Woman of God is a triumphal procession dispersing the fragrance of knowledge of Christ, a sweet perfume, everywhere.

> *Memory Verse*
>
> *I can do everything through him who gives me strength.*
>
> *Philippians 4:13 NIV*

Okay, ladies, Confident Women of God are righteous women of God, growing in grace, and growing in understanding, and we are not only hearers, but doers of His Word.

READ: EXODUS 2:4, 7; NUMBERS 12:1-2; MICAH 6:4; EXODUS 15: 20-21

T/F

_____ Miriam was a devoted sister and served with Moses and Aaron and was on the first leadership team.

_____ Miriam was not devoted to God and ministry.

_____ Once Miriam made a mistake, she never sang again.

_____ Miriam is the epitome of where sisterhood, singleness, senior-hood, servant leadership, songstress, and sainthood came forth with spectacular energy!

CONFIDENT WOMEN OF GOD, on whose shoulders we stand are many in and out of the Bible. I cherish the memories of our Great Women who have gone on before us. It's a wonderful thing to study our history and to celebrate CONFIDENT WOMEN DESIGNED BY ALMIGHTY GOD.

HARRIET TUBMAN (1820-1913) The "Moses" of her people. She often said, "I always tole God, I'm gwine (going) to hole stiddy on you, an you've got to see me through."

As we share in this study, I want to challenge you to remember the past. Sisters, life places before us many possibilities, some are good, and many are bad. Each of us must decide for ourselves which way to go.

There's a song that I love to sing, and it has become my life's theme: "If I can help somebody as I pass along, then my living will not be in vain." My Sisters in Christ, we face a struggling world in which changes are all around us, we witness disasters on every side. There are planes going down like never before, diseases are rampart, wars, rotten politics, tornadoes, hurricanes, floods, home foreclosures, fires, churches losing their zeal and so many other devastating things happening in our world.

We need to be the Confident Women of God that He made us to be. "Therefore, my dear brothers, stand firm. Let nothing, move you. Always give yourselves fully to the work of the Lord, because you know that your labor in the Lord is not in vain. (1 Corinthians 15:58)

THINK ON THESE THINGS:

1. How do you handle adversities in your life?

_____
_____
_____
_____
_____

2. Describe how you believe God designed us to function as Confident Women of God when bad things happen to us.

    _____

    _____

    _____

    _____

    _____

    _____

Let's take a look at the life of another Confident Woman of God, MARY MCLEOD BETHUNE (1875-1955), an African American teacher. Yes Women, it is true that little becomes much when placed in the Master's hands.

I'm proud to say today that according to history, Mary McLeod Bethune founded a Black College (Bethune-Cookman College) with "five little girls, a dollar and half and Faith in God.

THINK ON THESE THINGS: "I CAN DO EVERYTHING THROUGH HIM WHO GIVES ME

STRENGTH." (Philippians 4:13)

*   Who are you in Christ Jesus?

    _____

    _____

    _____

    _____

*   Do you have a dream inside of you waiting to be acted upon?

    _____

    _____

    _____

    _____

- What's keeping you from being confident in knowing that God means just what He says?

_____

_____

_____

_____

MARY GLENN SLEDD (August 31, 1916-April 25, 2005) - A CONFIDENT WOMAN DESIGNED BY ALMIGHTY GOD.

Mary Glenn Sledd is my Aunt Mary. She is my mother's sister who "took what she had and made the most of it." Aunt Mary greatly influenced my life. She never gave birth to a child, but raised her sisters and brothers as a teenager due to her mother and fathers early deaths. Throughout her life, she helped many people along the way with food, shelter and a little money here and there. She never received public assistance, but worked hard and prayed often.

Yes, she herself had many dark days, but found great satisfaction in encouraging others. She loved these words written by Robert Browning about optimism: "One who never turned his back but marched breast forward, Never doubted clouds would break, Never dreamed, though right were worsted, wrong would triumph, Held we fall to rise, are baffled to fight better, Sleep to wake." Robert Browning, Asolando, Epilogue

My Mom, her sisters and brothers always praised Aunt Mary for loving them and providing for them. No matter how bad life seemed, no matter how little money she had, no matter how tired she got, Mary Sledd always plowed on. She never knew what it was like to play as a child. She always said that a positive outlook, liking people and a firm faith in Almighty God kept her head above the water.

Aunt Mary served God, her church, community and family until death. She was a teacher in Paducah, KY, for 26 years and during those years she touched many lives. All of her sisters and brothers made her proud, and did well in life. Yes, I miss her, and will tell her story every time I get an opportunity.

As you continue this study, remember there's always a better day. There's always something positive for you, but you must believe in Almighty God who made you, and is able to keep you.

TAKE A LOOK AT YOURSELF TODAY:

SUGGESTED ACTIVITIES:

1. In your journal, spend time reflecting on yourself. Ask yourself the question, what would I want to leave behind for future generations?
2. Find a way to thank some woman in your life that has helped you along the way. Send a card, write a letter, send a flower, make a phone call, or simply find a way to say Thank You!

CONFIDENT WOMEN OF GOD, we must leave no one behind. Mary McLeod Bethune left a great legacy, and gave us an idea of what we can leave to others:

- I LEAVE YOU LOVE - Love builds
- I LEAVE YOU HOPE
- I LEAVE YOU THE CHALLENGE OF DEVELOPING CONFIDENCE IN ONE ANOTHER
- I LEAVE YOU A THIRST FOR EDUCATION
- I LEAVE YOU RESPECT FOR THE USES OF POWER
- I LEAVE YOU FAITH

SESSION TWO: CONFIDENT WOMEN OF GOD: PAST. PRESENT AND FUTURE

DAY FIVE: REVIEW, RESOLUTION, STRATEGIES

It is an awesome privilege to be given a mind to follow Christ: He gave us confidence. He gives us strength. He gives us comfort and guidance: He will complete the good work that He began in us. We are able to see ourselves how He sees. We are fragrant offerings to the world to share the gospel in an infinite, number of ways depending who we are in Christ Jesus. No more study this week.

Memory Verse
I can do everything through him who gives me strength.
Philippians 4:13 NIV

STRATEGIC THINKING & ACTION PLANNING

HOW HAS "CONFIDENT WOMEN OF GOD: PAST, PRESENT, FUTURE" IMPACTED YOU? HAS YOUR MIND OR HEART CHANGED?

LIST TWO OR THREE STRATEGIES FOR IMPLEMENTING LESSONS LEARNED IN "CONFIDENT WOMEN OF GOD: PAST, PRESENT, & FUTURE"?

GROUP DISCUSSION

1. As a group, decide how to summarize the lessons learned in three minutes.
2. Share your personal strategies, and discuss how "the group" will implement the lessons learned in Session 2, CONFIDENT WOMEN OF GOD: PAST, PRESENT, & FUTURE.
3. Make sure that everyone in the group has memorized Philippians 1:6, and Philippians 4:13.

"being confident of this, that He who began a good work in you will carry it on to completion until the day of Christ Jesus" Philippians 1:6

ARE YOU ABLE TO HELP OTHERS USING THE MATERIAL LEARNED IN "CONFIDENT WOMEN OF GOD: PAST, PRESENT, FUTURE"? PLEASE EXPLAIN.

PREPARE A CREATIVE PIECE (PICTURE, PAINTING, SHORT STORY, POEM), REFLECTING ANY ASPECT OF *SESSION TWO:* CONFIDENT WOMEN OF GOD, PAST, PRESENT, & FUTURE, FOR ANY DAY.

SESSION THREE: CONFIDENT WOMEN IN THE BIBLE

Day 1 Hannah and Abigail

Day 2 Lydia, Phoebe, Dorcas

Day 3 Mary, Mother of Jesus, Elizabeth

Day 4 Queen of Sheba, The Daughters of Zelophehad

Day 5 Review, Resolution & Strategies

SESSION THREE: <u>**CONFIDENT WOMEN IN THE BIBLE**</u>

Praise Him! Praise Him! Jesus, our blessed Redeemer! Is your heart rejoicing? Are you consistently conscious that you can do everything through Him who gives you strength? We thank Almighty God for women in the Bible who serve as models for us today. Yes, we have shoulders to stand on from the past, sisters to stand beside in the present, and young girls and teens to lead into the future.

MEMORY VERSE: "MY HEART REJOICES IN THE LORD; IN THE LORD MY HORN IS LIFTED HIGH." 1 Samuel 2:1b (NIV)

The word horn in this verse comes from the Hebrew word meaning strength. I pray that you will find the strength to complete this study! Bring a friend, and remember that each session builds on the next session, but also can stand alone.

Be creative! During this session, some of your classmates might want to present a play about Confident Women in the Bible. You may have women in the study to represent one of the women that you will study in the Bible. For instance, one of the women may represent Hannah. She will dress like Hannah, and give some of the information she gathered concerning Hannah.

Abigail, Lydia, Phoebe, Dorcas, Mary-Mother of Jesus, Elizabeth, Queen of Sheba, and the Daughters of Zelophehad.

SESSION THREE: <u>**CONFIDENT WOMEN IN THE BIBLE**</u>

DAY ONE: <u>HANNAH & ABIGAIL</u>

<u>Please write Philippians 1:6 below:</u>

_____

_____

_____

_____

<u>Hannah – A Woman of Grace Who Knew How to Love</u>, is one of our most well known women of the Bible. Samuel was her first born, and she leaves him at the temple.

<u>READ</u>: 1 Samuel 1; 1 Samuel 2

<u>TELL HANNAH'S STORY</u>, Using Your Own Words

_____

_____

_____

_____

_____

_____

_____

_____

Memory Verse
"My heart rejoices in the LORD; in the LORD my horn is lifted high."
1 Samuel 2:1b (NIV)

<u>DESCRIBE</u> Hannah

_____

_____

_____

_____

"being confident of this, that He who began a good work in you will carry it on to completion until the day of Christ Jesus" Philippians 1:6

<u>COMPARE</u>: I Samuel 2: I -10 and Luke 1:46-55

T/F

_____ Hannah and Mary were rejoicing.
_____ Hannah and Mary were complaining that the Lord delivered them from their enemies.
_____ Hannah and Mary recognized God as their deliverer.

<u>REFLECTIONS:</u>

1. Are you sympathetic and sensitive to those around you who do not have children? Do you flaunt your favor, position, education?
2. How does the fact that your children and grandchildren are gifts to you from God impact your parenting or grand-parenting?
3. Is someone constantly taunting you, teasing you, or looking down at you? How do you respond?

The name HANNAH means grace in Hebrew. Her song of praise suggests that she was a prophetess, an encourager. She is known for her pain, reverence of God, prayer, faith, sacrifice, glory, vision and growth.

<u>ABIGAIL - A woman with God's own poise</u> was married to a man whose name meant fool and folly. Abigail's name indicates that she knew who she was and whose she was.

<u>READ</u> 1 Samuel 25, and fill in the blanks. We used the NIV version, but any should do.

Verse 3: His name was Nabal and his wife's name was _____ She was an _____ and _____ woman, but her husband, a Calebite, was surly and _____ in his dealings.

Ans - Abigail, intelligent, beautiful, mean

Verse 18 _____ lost no _____.
She took two hundred loaves of bread, two skins of
wine, five dressed sheep, five seahs of roasted grain,
a hundred cakes of raisins and two hundred cakes of
pressed figs, and _____ them on donkeys.

Ans - Abigail, time, loaded

Verse 23: When _____ saw
David, she _____ got off her donkey and
_____ down before David with her face to the ground.

Ans - Abigail, quickly, bowed

Verse 42 Abigail _____ got on a donkey and, attended
by her five _____, went with David's messengers and
became his _____.

Ans - quickly, maids, wife

Describe Nabal in 1 Samuel 25

_____
_____
_____
_____

EXPLAIN: Why did David save Nabal's life?

_____
_____
_____
_____

> ### Memory Verse
>
> *"My heart rejoices*
> *in the LORD; in*
> *the LORD my horn*
> *is lifted high."*
>
> *1 Samuel 2:1b*
> *(NIV)*

31

SESSION THREE: <u>CONFIDENT WOMEN IN THE BIBLE</u>

DAY TWO: <u>DORCAS, LYDIA, PHOEBE</u>

<u>Please write Philippians 1:6 below:</u>

_____

_____

_____

_____

<u>DORCAS - A WOMAN WHO PRACTICED HER FAITH</u>

The name Dorcas and its Greek form Tabitha, means gazelle. The gazelle has antelopes, known for their ability to move quickly in case of danger appears nervous and jumpy, as are deer. The gazelle is often used for symbolisms for grace and elegance. In the Bible, they were symbols of love and beauty for the Hebrews (Song of Solomon 2:9, 17). They were also considered a major game animal, regularly supplied at Solomon's table (1 Kings 4:23), though they were difficult to catch because of their swiftness (2 Sam. 2:18; 1 Chron. 12:8).

> *Memory Verse*
>
> *"My heart rejoices in the LORD; in the LORD my horn is lifted high."*
>
> *1 Samuel 2:1b (NIV)*

<u>READ CHAPTER</u>: ACTS 9:36-41.

T/F

_____ Dorcas was a disciple that did not help the poor or perform any works of charity.

_____ Death was of great concern to those she lived among.

_____ Dorcas studied and applied the teachings of Jesus.

READ CHAPTER 9 IN ITS ENTIRETY

Who was on the scene looking for Christians to kill?

_____

What happened to Saul before he could get to Peter or Dorcas?

_____

_____

_____

What happened because of God working through Peter, Dorcas, and the people they served?

_____

_____

LYDIA - A CHRISTIAN PROFESSIONAL WOMAN

READ ACTS 16

Who was expecting to find a place of prayer, but instead sat down to speak to the women that had gathered there? _____

What did Lydia, a worshiper of God do for living? _____

> *Memory Verse*
>
> *"My heart rejoices in the LORD; in the LORD my horn is lifted high."*
>
> *1 Samuel 2:1b (NIV)*

How did Lydia respond to the message? _____

_____

Who did Lydia invite into her home and why? _____

_____

What did Lydia have to do to get them there? _____

_____

Using your own words describe Lydia.

_____

_____

_____

_____

Lydia was a confident woman of God, woman of rank, head of household (widowed or unmarried), hospitable, woman of Thyatira in Lydia, who at Philippi became Paul's first European convert and gave him hospitality, with Silas and Luke. Since the early Christians were meeting by the riverside, it is thought that Lydia's home was the place of the first church in Thyatira. First persuaded, then persuasive, Lydia, worshipped God.

REFLECTIONS

1. Is your heart filled with God's love and goodness, a heart intent on doing good works for Him and His people?
2. Are you influencing others to follow Christ?
3. How open is your heart and your home to minister to others?

PHOEBE - A PLAIN WOMAN WITH A RESPONSIBLE HEART, name means radiant.

READ Romans 16:1-2

FILL IN THE BLANKS (We're using NIV)

I _____to you our sister Phoebe, a _____ of the church in Cenchrea, I ask you to receive her in the Lord in a way _____ of the _____ give her any help she may need from you, for she has been a _____ help to _____ people, including me.

> *Memory Verse*
>
> *"My heart rejoices in the LORD; in the LORD my horn is lifted high."*
>
> *1 Samuel 2:1b (NIV)*

<u>Ans -</u> commend, servant, worthy, saints, great, many

<u>READ</u> ROMANS 16: 1-16

<u>LIST</u> all the names of the women mentioned.

_____

_____

_____

_____

_____

_____

_____

<u>READ</u>: Romans 16:17-27

FILL IN THE BLANKS

Verse 17: I urge you, brothers, to _____ out for those who cause _____ and put _____ in your way that are _____ to the teaching you have learned. Keep away from them.

Ans - watch, divisions, obstacles, contrary.

Verse 19: Everyone has heard about your _____ so I am full of _____ over you; but I want you to be _____ about what is _____, and _____ about what is evil.

Ans - obedience, joy, wise, good, innocent

Verse 25: _____ to _____ who is able to establish _____ by my gospel and the proclamation of _____ Christ, according to the revelation of the mystery hidden for long ages past,

Ans - Now, Him, you, Jesus

SUGGESTED ACTIVITIES

1. If there is a man or woman in your church that functions as a trainer to you, show him or her appreciation.

2. Watch, pray, and turn away from divisions, obstacles, and anything contrary to the teachings of Jesus Christ.

3. Invite a minister of God into your home and show them some hospitality. Daughters are you

> **Memory Verse**
>
> *"My heart rejoices in the LORD; in the LORD my horn is lifted high."*
>
> *1 Samuel 2:1b*
> *(NIV)*

convinced that God is able to establish you by His gospel? Certainly, we could say so about Phoebe. Paul references her as "our sister", she is considered a devoted and committed member of the family of God. He mentions her as a servant of the church in Cenchria, which is the honored title from which our English words for deacon, deaconess, and minister come. Servants of the church serve any and all in the church. Finally, Phoebe is mentioned as a helper. In classical Greek, helper refers to a trainer in the Olympic Games who stood by to see that athletes were properly trained, rightly girded for competition. Today, the person is called a coach or trainer in athletics. Helper literally means "one who stands by in case of need."

SESSION THREE: <u>**CONFIDENT WOMEN IN THE BIBLE**</u>

DAY THREE: <u>MARY, MOTHER OF JESUS, ELIZABETH</u>

<u>Please write Philippians 1:6 below:</u>

_____

_____

_____

_____

READ: Matthew 1, 2; Luke 1, 2

ANSWER:

Who is the mother of Jesus? _____

Which cousin does she visit? _____

What does the angel tell Mary? _____

How does Elizabeth greet Mary? _____

Where is Mary when Jesus entrusts her to the care of his beloved disciple?

_____

In what ways did Mary act as a typical mother towards her son?

_____

_____

How would you describe Mary?

_____

_____

Mary, our beloved mother of God, was a young woman chosen. She is to this day, blessed among women for her humility, obedience, and reverence for God. Mary had the heart of a handmaiden (servant), and an attitude of acceptance.

"being confident of this, that He who began a good work in you will carry it on to completion until the day of Christ Jesus" Philippians 1:6

READ: Luke 1:46-55

REFLECTIONS

1. How do you handle shocking news or unfair circumstances? Does anything keep you from saying, "let it be to me according to Your Word."

2. What could you do to learn more about the character of our trustworthy God?

ELIZABETH - A WOMAN FREE FROM DOUBT, an older cousin to Mary was of priestly descent and Godly character. She was barren until her elder years: Her name is derived from a Hebrew name meaning "my God is oath."

READ: Luke 1

T/F

_____Elizabeth was the mother of John the Baptist.
_____Elizabeth was jealous of Mary.
_____Elizabeth complained about her barrenness?
_____Elizabeth withdrew from public life for five months?

Tell Elizabeth's story of God in her life using your own words.

_____
_____
_____
_____
_____
_____
_____
_____
_____

SUGGESTED ACTIVITIES

1. Rank yourself on a scale of 1-10 on how willing you are to accept the life that God has given you, and the path He is leading you to take.
2. Rank yourself on a scale of 1-10 on how open you are to receive and to comfort a woman of God who appears to have a bigger assignment from God than you.
3. Take a step towards trusting in God today. Whenever in doubt, fear, or anxiety, say "let it be to me according to your word."

> *Memory Verse*
>
> *"My heart rejoices in the LORD; in the LORD my horn is lifted high."*
>
> *1 Samuel 2:1b (NIV)*

CHECK ALL THE DESCRIPTIVE WORDS THAT YOU THINK APPLY TO ELIZABETH

_____ wise
_____ haughty
_____ friend
_____ humble
_____ faithful
_____ talked about
_____ jealous
_____ mature
_____ hopeful
_____ visionary
_____ stuck-up
_____ stuck-up
_____ envious

> CAN YOU THINK OF OTHER WORDS TO DESCRIBE "ELIZABETH?"

Mary and Elizabeth - Mary a young woman chosen, and Elizabeth a woman free from doubt. One was young, and the other old, one mother of Jesus, the other to the one not worthy to wear the sandals of Jesus. They loved each other, they loved their children, and most importantly, they loved and were obedient to God

SESSION THREE: **CONFIDENT WOMEN IN THE BIBLE**

DAY FOUR: <u>QUEEN OF SHEBA, DAUGHTERS OF ZELOPHEHAD</u>

A confident woman of God functions as servant doing works of charity for the poor; she may function as a servant in the church meeting the needs of all. She may function as a host caring for other ministers of the gospel. She may host church or studies in her own home. She may or may not be beautiful according to worldly standards, but she is definitely beautiful in God's eyes.

Please write Philippians 1:6 below:

> *Memory Verse*
>
> *"My heart rejoices in the LORD; in the LORD my horn is lifted high."*
>
> *1 Samuel 2:1b (NIV)*

_____

_____

_____

_____

THE QUEEN OF SHEBA - A WOMAN WITH A BEAUTIFUL MIND, is a well-known confident woman in the Bible. This royal woman's name, Sheba, refers to a geographical region or group of people; the number seven, and the word oath.

COMPARE 1 Kings 10:1-10, and 1 Chronicles 9

<u>T/F</u>

_____ The Queen came to see Solomon because she had heard of his fame only.

_____ The Queen came bearing gifts but asked Solomon a lot of hard questions.

_____ Solomon appreciated the Queen's beautiful mind, and she admired his love for God, and his wisdom.

_____ Queen of Sheba left with far more gifts than she came.

WRITE: The Queen of Sheba Story in your own words.

_____

_____

_____

_____

_____

_____

REFLECTIONS

1. Do you have questions for the leaders of your church, your boss, etc.? List the people and the questions in your journal?
2. The Queen of Sheba was definitely a giver. On a scale of 1-20 rank yourself on your ability to give gifts of love and admiration to others.
3. Think of someone that you might approach bearing gifts.

> *Memory Verse*
>
> *"My heart rejoices in the LORD; in the LORD my horn is lifted high."*
>
> *1 Samuel 2:1b (NIV)*

THE DAUGHTERS OF ZELOPHEHAD - FIVE WOMEN WHO CAME TOGETHER TO TAKE CARE OF BUSINESS ... LAND OWNERS, names were Mahlah, Noah, Hoglah, Milcah, and Tirzah. These five sisters were descendants of the tribe of Manasseh.

Mahlah - the eldest of 5 daughters name means "disease or weak."

Noah - next to the eldest of the 5 daughters of Zelophehad in the time of the exodus, means "motion".

Hoolah - 3rd of 5 daughters of Zelophehad, means partridge. A partridge, like a hen is a "caller," preferring to run or walk than fly.

Milcah – the 4th daughter's name means queen.

Tirza - the youngest daughters of Zelophehad, means favorable.

READ: Numbers 27:1-11; Joshua 17:3-6

WRITE: The Daughters of Zelophehad Story Using Your Own Words

_____

_____

_____

_____

_____

_____

_____

_____

_____

_____

_____

_____

_____

T/F

_____ Zelophehad daughters were not afraid to go before the lawmakers to petition for positive change.

_____ The Lord was on their side.

_____ Law's and cultural climates may change but our loving God never does!

> *Memory Verse*
>
> *"My heart rejoices in the LORD; in the LORD my horn is lifted high."*
>
> *1 Samuel 2:1b*
> *(NIV)*

ACTIVITIES

1. If there is something of yours that you have unclaimed, go and get it.
2. If you have questions of someone, go and ask them.

Some people may consider the Queen of Sheba and the Daughters of Zelophehad as out of the box. Picture the Queen of Sheba followed by an entourage of servants bearing gifts for the most powerful and wise man in the world. Though beautiful, she came asking tough questions as perhaps a

lawyer or judge would. She wanted to confirm that everything that she heard about this man and His God were true. She was well accepted and left with more than she came. Now that is confidence!

The Daughters of Zelophehad, as a group were awesome! As their names imply, they had different strengths and weaknesses and even operated out of birth order. The oldest was probably sick, the second was a mover, the third, was more settled on the ground. The fourth daughter obviously had a queenly demeanor, and may have been the leader, while the last daughter was considered favorable. It is interesting to note that she was not considered "spoiled" as most youngest children are today. These sisters came before the patriarchs to take care of business, to get what was theirs, and they accomplished their mission.

SESSION THREE: <u>**CONFIDENT WOMEN IN THE BIBLE**</u>

DAY FIVE: <u>REVIEW, RESOLUTION, STRATEGIES</u>

Do you know how to love? Do you possess the poise of God? Are you a woman of courage? Are you free from doubt? Do you practice your faith? Are you a professional woman? Are you a plain woman with a responsible heart? Are you a woman with a beautiful mind? Are you able to come together to take care of business? The word of God gives us plenty of examples of confident women of God of all personalities, demeanors, professions, status, single, married, barren, sick, and well. Despite all, can you say you are a Confident Woman of God? You may not be where you want to be, but remember that He who began a good work in you shall see it through to completion. Know that He that is in you is greater than He that is in the world, and rejoice! Rejoice and blow your horn of strength. You are a daughter of the King of kings, Lord of lords. I am running, running with Jesus.

This week let's take a look at the second stanza of our resolution:

> I am Resolved to be a Confident Woman of God: Realizing that God's way is the only way. In the natural order of His creation there is always harmony, never confusion; always peace, never strife; always abundance, never lack; always good, never evil; always love, never hate.

<u>READ GALATIONS 5:22-24</u> in your own bibles. The Amplified Version says it this way:

But the fruit of the [Holy] Spirit [the work which His presence within accomplishes] is love, joy (gladness), peace, patience (an even temper, forbearance), kindness, goodness (benevolence), faithfulness, gentleness (meekness, humility), self-control (self-restraint, continence). Against such things there is no law that can bring a charge. And those who belong to Christ Jesus (the Messiah) have crucified the flesh (the godless human nature) with its passions and appetites and desires.

Pray for the fruit of the Holy Spirit to manifest itself in you, through you, in your homes, churches, workplace, in your relationships. Recite the Resolution with your group. Have you posted it? Please make sure to share it with another woman, saved or unsaved.

STRATEGIC THINKING & ACTION PLANNING

HOW HAS "CONFIDENT WOMEN OF THE BIBLE" IMPACTED YOU? HAS YOUR MIND OR HEART CHANGED?

> *Memory Verse*
>
> *"My heart rejoices in the LORD; in the LORD my horn is lifted high."*
>
> *1 Samuel 2:1b (NIV)*

LIST TWO OR THREE STRATEGIES FOR IMPLEMENTING LESSONS LEARNED IN "CONFIDENT WOMEN OF THE BIBLE"?

GROUP DISCUSSION

1. As a group, decide how to summarize the lessons learned in three minutes.
2. Share your personal strategies, and discuss how "the group" will implement the lessons learned in Session 3, CONFIDENT WOMEN OF THE BIBLE.
3. Make sure that everyone in the group has memorized Philippians 1:6, and 1 Samuel 2:1b.

ARE YOU ABLE TO HELP OTHERS USING THE MATERIAL LEARNED IN "CONFIDENT WOMEN OF THE BIBLE"? PLEASE EXPLAIN.

PREPARE A CREATIVE PIECE (PICTURE, PAINTING, SHORT STORY, POEM) REFLECTING ANY ASPECT OF SESSION TWO: CONFIDENT WOMEN OF IN THE BIBLE, FOR ANY DAY.

SESSION FOUR: SELF-ESTEEM & SELF-ASSURANCE

Day 1: Loving God, Yourself and Others

Day 2: Being True to Yourself & Others

Day 3: Jealousy & Envy/Letting Go of the Past

Day 4: Gratitude & Attitude/Live to give & Choose To Be Happy

Day 5: Review, Resolution & Strategies

Let's take a look at where we've been as we prepare to move forward:

- In Session One, we learned who and whose you are, and the importance and power of prayer.
- In Session Two, we discovered the significance of our mind in relationship to our faith, what it means to be a woman of God, when, where and why confidence is necessary, and shared descriptions and examples of Confident Women of God.
- In Session Three, we shared examples of Confident Women in the Bible and provided examples of humble, bold, courageous and obedient women during biblical days.
- In this Session Four, we will study all about our personal relationships with Almighty God… the young, old, married, single, uneducated, educated, professionals, stay-at-home moms that are happy and those that are unhappy. In this session, we want to put feet to our faith.

I AM, I CAN, I WILL

You need courage to say, "I AM. I am a Child of God, and I am convinced that He wants me to be a Confident Woman. You don't need to be smart. You may need more knowledge, more training to sharpen your skills, read more, pray more, but God has placed inside of us everything that we need to be who He wants us to be. You need to tell yourself and others, "I CAN". "I can do everything through him who gives me strength" (Philippians 4:13). We must say it, and believe it. Our power and confidence is in God, not in ourselves.

Now it is time to move out and say "I WILL". Here is where you run the risk of success or failure. Remember, there is no failure in God. I remember enrolling in Seminary after being out of college for years. I was the age of 38 years, the mother of a 2 year old and a 15 year old. Plus, my husband was Pastor of a growing church. I went 3 days a week, and had to drive approximately 50 miles one way. Some said that I wouldn't make it-all odds were against me-a woman taking a risk in a so-called man's world. I realized that the only real failure, was failure to try. My mother often said, "Nothing beats a failure, but a trial." So, in spite of tears and some difficult days, I pressed on, and in three years I graduated from Golden Gate Baptist Theological Seminary in Mill Valley. Praise God from whom all blessings flow! As a result, I've been blessed to help my husband build a strong Christian Education Department/Discipleship Division. God never fails! My son who was then 15 years old is now my Pastor. He succeeded his father as pastor. The younger son is our percussionist. When we decide to do things God's way, He has a way of leading us through it all.

SEVEN POTENTIALS FOR A CONFIDENT WOMAN OF GOD

1. Enlarge your vision (Isaiah 54:2)
2. Develop a Healthy Self-Image (Ephesians 2:10)
3. Discover the Power of your Thoughts and Your Words (Philippians 4:8)
4. Let Go of the Past (Philippians 3:13)
5. Find Strength Through Adversity (Romans 8:28)
6. Live to Give (Proverbs 11:25)
7. Choose to be Happy (Philippians 4:12)

SESSION FOUR: **SELF-ESTEEM & SELF-ASSURANCE**

DAY ONE: LOVING GOD, YOURSELF AND OTHERS

WHAT DOES LOVE HAVE TO DO WITH IT? The answer is EVERYTHING! Too many women of God have low self-esteem and are not self-assured. They look like they have it all, they act like they have it, they dress with the latest fashions, drive the most expensive cars, but it's all a lie. We have become quite proficient at wearing emotional masks. Self-esteem means believing in one's self, having self-respect. Let us look at respect which means relationally deserving of high regard. Sometimes we value other people over ourselves. Self-assurance means confidence in oneself, or in one's own ability or talent.

Confident Women of God know that self-esteem and self-assurance are all about Love and Confidence in Jesus Christ.

Please read and explain the following passage - Matthew 22:37-39:

_____

_____

_____

_____

_____

_____

_____

READ: 2 Corinthians 5:14-15; 1 John 4:17-21

EXPLAIN:

What does Christ's love compel us to do?

_____

How did God show his love among us?

_____

"being confident of this, that He who began a good work in you will carry it on to completion until the day of Christ Jesus" Philippians 1:6

_____

_____

_____

_____

Does fear affect our ability to experience love?

_____

_____

_____

_____

_____

READ ISAIAH 43: 1-5

CHECK ALL THAT APPLY

_____ Fear not for God has redeemed you.

_____ You have not been summoned by God, for you are not His.

_____ When you pass through waters, rivers, and fire you will be safe.

_____ God loves you, you are precious and honored in his sight.

_____ You should not be afraid is because God is not thinking about you, nor your children.

REFLECTIONS

1. On a scale of 1-10, how self-assured are you? Write in your journal why you feel the way you do.
2. Does your esteem or assurance in your gifts, talents, and abilities depend on your own thinking or someone else's? Write in your journal three to ten people that make you feel good about yourself and/ or reinforces a healthy self-esteem and self-assurance.

> *Memory Verse*
>
> *If I rise on the wings of the dawn, if I settle on the far side of the sea, even there your hand will guide me, your right hand will hold me fast.*
>
> *Psalm 139:9-10 NIV*

3. Write in journal ten things you would do if you were capable or if you had the chance?

SUGGESTED ACTIVITES

Take responsibility for your own self-esteem and self-assurance by preparing an arsenal of God's word to bolster you when you are under attack by the critique within, others, and Satan himself.

Choose relationships wisely.

Take a risk and do at least one of the things you would do if you were capable or if you had the chance.

SESSION FOUR: **SELF-ESTEEM & SELF-ASSURANCE**

DAY TWO: <u>BEING TRUE TO YOURSELF AND OTHERS</u>

Admit where you are, so you can move forward in healing and health.

<u>Please write Philippians 1:6 below:</u>

_____

_____

_____

_____

READ: Psalm 51:6

T/F

_____ God desires truth in the inner parts.

_____ The inner parts refer to our outward exterior.

_____ Inner parts and inmost place are very similar if not the same.

_____ Truth and wisdom are interrelated.

<u>READ</u>: John 8: 31-32

EXPLAIN: What will knowing the truth about **<u>YOU</u>** do for **<u>YOU</u>**?

_____

_____

READ: Romans 8:35-39

List the things that cannot separate you from the love of Christ.

1	
2	
3	
4	
5	
6	
7	
8	
9	
10	
11	
12	
13	
14	
15	
16	
17	
18	

T/F

_____ Nakedness = truth
_____ Nor anything else = nothing

"being confident of this, that He who began a good work in you will carry it on to completion until the day of Christ Jesus" Philippians 1:6

REFLECTIONS

1. List in your journal your areas of weakness spiritually, emotionally, educationally, etc. Decide which are harming you and others the most.
2. List in your journal your areas of strength. Decide which are the most helpful to you and others.
3. List missed opportunities because of your lack of self-esteem or self-confidence. Decide which ones you would still want to do if you had the chance.

> *Memory Verse*
>
> *If I rise on the wings of the dawn, if I settle on the far side of the sea, even there your hand will guide me, your right hand will hold me fast.*
>
> *Psalm 139:9-10*
> *NIV*

SUGGESTED ACTIVITIES

1. Research ways o decrease weakness that you decided were most harmful, i.e., creative ways to get the same thing accomplished, more training, delegation, etc
2. Research ways to improve your strengths: education, classes, pair up with someone of similar strengths, etc.
3. Do the things you still want to do and LET THE OTHERS GO!

SESSION FOUR: <u>**SELF-ESTEEM & SELF-ASSURANCE**</u>

DAY THREE: <u>JEALOUSY & ENVY – LET IT GO!</u>

Jealousy and envy are just plain evil. As human beings, we need to constantly, be on watch about jealousy and envy within our own selves. Confident Women of God run away, turn away, watch out for it because they know from reading God's word that it is not what God desires from his people. Confident Women of God cannot allow themselves to be tricked into jealousy or envy.

<u>Please write Philippians 1:6 below:</u>

_____

_____

_____

_____

We have mentioned jealousy and envy several times throughout this study because it is antithetical to confidence.. Paul was in prison when He wrote this letter. Did he seem jealous? No, in fact he was joyful and appreciated that the servants of Philippi were continuing the work of the Lord.

<u>READ</u>: Philippians 4:1

EXPLAIN: What did Paul call the people in Philippi?

_____

_____

We have too many examples of the devastating effects of jealousy beginning with Cain of Abel, Joseph's brothers with Joseph; Sarah, of Hagar, Saul, of David; Joab, of Abner, Nathan of Adonijah, Ephraimites, of Gideon, the brother of the prodigal son, and between Israel and Judah.

READ: 1 Samuel 18:8-30; 1 Samuel 19:8-24; 1 Samuel 20:24-30.

Who are the characters in these verses and what are their relationships to one another?

_____

_____

_____

_____

_____

Describe what happened in this story?

_____

_____

_____

_____

_____

_____

_____

READ: Ps. 56:4

EXPLAIN: If you are jealous or envious of another, or they are of you, then why should you not be concerned about it?

_____

_____

READ: Proverbs 3:5-6

LIST three conditions for making **YOUR** path straight. (Hints included in parentheses.)

1. _____(heart).
2. _____(understanding).
3. _____(acknowledge).

READ: Romans 12:1-2

EXPLAIN: Where should our eyes be focused?

_____

READ: John 10:10 – "The thief comes only to steal and kill and destroy; I have come that they may have life, and have it to the full."

EXPLAIN: What does self-esteem and self-assurance have to do with a full life?

_____

_____

_____

T/F

_____ The thief is doing his job when you have low self-esteem.

_____ Your body only includes those parts that you can see such as your arms, legs, etc.

_____You honor God only be keeping your physical body fit.

READ: Exodus 3:12; Hebrew 12:28; Rev. 19:10; Rev. 22:9

T/F

_____ God desires us to worship one another.

_____Worship one another.

REFLECTIONS

1. One of the best ways to overcome jealous and envy is to watch for it in yourself and pray about it. Pray to God to improve your own self-esteem and self-assurance.
2. Another way to avoid jealousy and envy is by not having more respect for others than you do yourself. God tells us to "Worship God." How could worshipping others lead to jealousy and envy?

SUGGESTED ACTIVITIES

1. Keep your journal with you, every time you feel a tinge of jealousy or envy coming up on you, write down date, time, over whom and what, and why?
2. While you have your journal with you, note whenever you value someone's opinion over what God's Word says, or in absence of God's Word what you think?

SESSION FOUR: <u>**SELF-ESTEEM & SELF-ASSURANCE**</u>

DAY FOUR: <u>GRATITUDE & ATTITUDE/LIVING TO GIVE & CHOOSING TO BE HAPPY</u>

It is very difficult to have low self-esteem, and lack self-assurance when you focus on all that God is, all that He has brought you through to be a confident woman of God.

<u>Please write Philippians 1:6 below:</u>

_____

_____

_____

_____

READ: Romans 12:3:

EXPLAIN: Instead of thinking more highly of ourselves than we should, how should we think of ourselves?

_____

_____

_____

EXPLAIN: Does Paul seem grateful for something? If so what is he grateful for and why?

_____

_____

READ: Hebrews 12:28; 1 Corinthians 16:8; Psalm 100

CHECK ALL THAT APPLY

Since we have received a kingdom that cannot be shaken, we should not allow our self-esteem and self-assurance be shaken.

_____ Our esteem and assurance come from our confidence in Jesus Christ.

_____ It is appropriate to worship God with reverence and awe.

_____ We should not tell anyone what He has done for us.

_____ We are His people, the sheep of His pasture.

_____ The love of the Lord endures forever.

_____ Confident Women of God sing sad songs.

READ 1 Corinthians 15:57-58. FILL IN THE BLANKS

1 Cor 15:57-58 (NIV) But _____ be to God! He gives us the _____ through our Lord Jesus Christ. Therefore, my dear brothers, _____ firm. Let _____ move you. Always give _____ fully to the work of the Lord, because you know that your labor in the Lord is not in vain.

Ans - thanks, victory, stand, nothing, yourselves,

READ: 1 Thess. 5:18: give _____ in _____ _____ , for this is _____ _____ for _____ in Christ_____ .

Ans - thanks, all circumstances, God's will, you, Jesus

READ: JOSHUA 1:6 and FILL IN THE BLANKS

Be _____ and _____ , because _____ will _____ these _____ to _____ the land I swore to their forefathers to give them.

Ans - strong, courageous, you, lead, people, inherit

READ: Job 11:13-20

LIST four conditions God is asking of us (I'll put hints in parentheses).

1. _____(devote).
2. _____(stretch).
3. _____(put away).
4. _____(keep).

Oftentimes God will give us conditional promises. This is one of them. You are able to distinguish a conditional promise by the word "then."

CHECK all that apply if you do the four above:

_____ You will lift up your face without shame.
_____ You will stand firm and without fear.
_____ You will forget your trouble, recalling it only as waters gone by.
_____ Life will be brighter than noonday and darkness will become like morning.
_____ You will be secure.
_____ You will have hope.
_____ You will take your rest in safety.
_____ Many will court your favor.

STRATEGIC THINKING & ACTION PLANNING

HOW HAS "SELF-ESTEEM & SELF-ASSURANCE" IMPACTED YOU? HAS YOUR MIND OR HEART CHANGED?

Memory Verse

If I rise on the wings of the dawn, if I settle on the far side of the sea, even there your hand will guide me, your right hand will hold me fast.

Psalm 139:9-10 NIV

LIST TWO OR THREE ACTIVITIES OR STRATEGIES THAT YOU ARE USING TO APPLY THE LESSONS LEARNED IN "SELF-ESTEEM & SELF-ASSURANCE."

GROUP DISCUSSION

1. As a group, decide how to summarize the lessons learned in three minutes.
2. Share your personal strategies, and discuss how "the group" will implement the lessons learned in SESSION FOUR, 'SELF-ESTEEM & SELF-ASSURANCE."
3. Make sure that everyone in the group has memorized Philippians 1:6, and Psalm 139:9-10

ARE YOU ABLE TO HELP OTHERS USING THE "SELF-ESTEEM &
JEALOUSY", SESSION? PLEASE EXPLAIN.

PREPARE A CREATIVE PIECE (PICTURE, PAINTING, SHORT STORY,
POEM) REFLECTING ANY ASPECT OF SESSION FOUR: "SELF-
ESTEEM & SELF-ASSURANCE."

Conclusion

A believer's steadfastness for this life as well as confidence for eternity rest solely on the promises of God's Word:

"For all the promises of God in him are yea, and in him Amen, unto the glory of God by us." 2 Corinthians 1:20

"When you pass through the waters, I will be with you; and when you pass through the rivers, they will not sweep over you. When you walk through the fire, you will not be burned;" Isaiah 43:2

"The Lord is nigh unto them that are of a broken heart; and saveth such as be of a contrite spirit." Psalms 34:18

"Cast thy burden upon the lord, and he shall sustain thee; he shall never suffer the righteous to be moved." Psalms 55:22

Confident Women of Almighty God, I leave you with the words of a wonderful hymn. It reminds me often of my dependence upon the promises of Almighty God. The hymn is entitled "Standing on the Promises" and was written and composed by Russell Kelso Carter in 1886. This hymn has been widely used in churches and crusades around the world. Read with me the wonderful words of this hymn:

1. Standing on the promises of Christ my King, Thro eternal ages let His praises ring; Glory in the highest, I will shout and sing, Standing on the promises of God.
2. Standing on the promises that cannot fail, When the howling storms of doubt and fear assail, By the living Word of God I shall prevail, Standing on the promises of God.

3. Standing on the promises of Christ the Lord, Bound to Him eternally by love's strong cord, Overcoming daily with the Spirit's sword, Standing on the promises of God.
4. Standing on the promises I cannot fall, listening every moment to the Spirit's call, Resting in my Savior, as my all in all, Standing on the promises of God.

Chorus.

Standing, standing, Standing on the promises of God my Savior; standing, standing, I'm standing on the promises of God.

A CONFIDENT WOMAN OF GOD
LIVING FREE DAY BY DAY

Lord Jesus Thank you for making me
I know that I was born to be free
As the birds fly in Your sky
My soul soars over and over, oh so high.

Getting to know You has been my life's dream
Sometimes, I get so excited about your goodness that I could scream.
Forgive me when I don't trust you as I should
You deserve all Praises, because You are so good.

Living Free is a dream come true
That's why I love to Glorify You.
Worshipping You in Spirit and in Truth is beyond explaining
That's why I try to avoid so much complaining.

Satisfied with Jesus is where I find myself to be
God designed me to be Free.
Sweeter and sweeter as the days go by
I will forever look to Jesus, my Lord and Savior on High

Thank you, Father for the Peace no other can give
When days are long and nights are dark, You give the reason to live
You give me peace in sickness and in health
You even give me peace in financial lows and financial wealth.

Experiencing Your Presence is divine intimacy with You
No one on earth could ever do what you do.
There's great comfort in knowing that You are always with me
No matter what the circumstances may be.

To be a Confident Woman, Designed by Almighty God is God-ordained
To be a Confident Woman, Designed by Almighty God is God-maintained
Go forth Women of God and let the winds guide you as you grow
God promised to be with you wherever you may go.